# THE ODD SQUAD
## LITTLE BOOK OF

# POO

## BY ALLAN PLENDERLEITH

℞

RAVETTE PUBLISHING

*First published in 2001 by*
*Ravette Publishing Limited*
*Unit 3, Tristar Centre*
*Star Road, Partridge Green*
*West Sussex RH13 8RA*

*Printed in Malta by Gutenberg Press*

*ISBN: 1 84161 096 8*

## POO No.1

# THE FIREBALL

HOT AND PAINFUL.
GOOD FOR REMOVING
UNSIGHTLY
BOTTOM HAIRS.

POO No.2

# THE
# CHOP-OFF

**POO IS CHOPPED OFF
HALF-WAY DUE TO PHONE
RINGING ETC.**

# POO No.3

# THE SWEETCORN

## THE MOST COLOURFUL AND ATTRACTIVE OF ALL POOS.

POO No.4

# THE JAGGY

CAUSED BY EATING TOO MANY CRISPS. MAY RESULT IN SURGERY.

# POO No.5

# THE
# STICKY

STICKS TO HAIRS.
REQUIRES HOURS OF
WIPING.

# THE
# VEGGIE

## LOOKS AND SMELLS EXACTLY LIKE A VEGGIE BURGER.

# POO No.7

# THE FIREHOSE

## MAINLY WATER-BASED. CREATES HUGE MESS.

## POO No.8

# THE CROQUETTES

CRISPY ON THE OUTSIDE WITH A LIGHT, FLUFFY CENTRE.

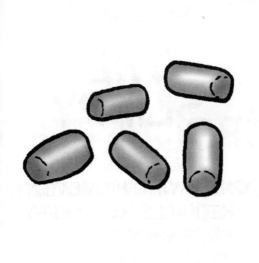

# POO No.9

# THE SLIPPY

SLIPS OUT IN
ONE SWIFT MOVEMENT.
REQUIRES NO WIPING.
PROBABLY THE BEST
POO IN THE WORLD.

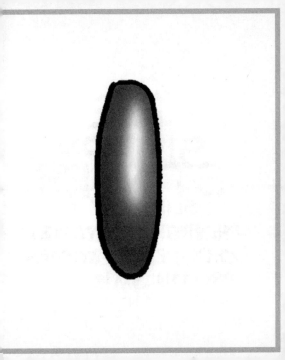

# POO No.10

# THE
# STINKER

**REEKS SO BAD YOU
DON'T EVEN RECOGNISE
THE SMELL.**

# POO No.11

# THE NEVERENDING STORY

AN AMAZING
ACHIEVEMENT.
MAY NEED TO STAND TO
ACCOMPLISH FULL LENGTH

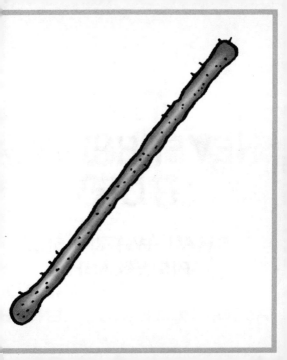

POO No.12

# THE
# BLIP

**SMALL BUT CAUSES
BIG SPLASH.**

POO No.13

# THE
# POPPETS

COME OUT LIKE
MACHINE-GUN BULLETS.

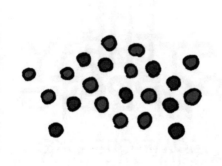

# POO No.14

# THE STEAMY HEAPY

PASSING THIS BABY IS AKIN TO GIVING BIRTH. WILL NEVER FLUSH.

## POO No.15

# BABY POO

LIKE NUCLEAR CABBAGE
ONLY DEADLIER.  DO NOT
LET IT COME IN CONTACT
WITH SKIN.

# POO No.16

# TEENAGE POO

JUST A BIG BALL OF LARD. MADE FROM A DIET OF BURGERS, PIZZAS AND CHOCOLATE. HIGHLY INFECTIOUS.

# POO No.17

# TWENTY SOMETHING POO

**POO IS GREEN DUE TO SUDDEN HEALTH KICK, BUT MORE VEG IN DIET MEANS SMELLIER POOS.**

# THIRTY SOMETHING POO

INCREASE IN DINNER PARTIES MEANS POOS BECOME DARKER AND RICHER IN QUALITY. THE BOUQUET IS ALMOST PLEASANT.

# FORTY SOMETHING POO

MIDDLE AGE SPREAD
SETS IN. POOS BECOME
HUGE SWOLLEN
MONSTROSITIES. JUST
LIKE THEIR BIG ARSES.

# POO No.20

# OLD AGED POO (OAP)

**POOS ARE GREY, WRINKLY, DRIED UP AND SMELL OF ROTTING FLESH.**

POO No.21

# THE INDIAN MEAL POO

A REAL HAIR BURNER.
SITTING DOWN WILL BE
IMPOSSIBLE FOR WEEKS.
KEEP A FIRE
EXTINGUISHER HANDY.

# POO No.22

# THE CHINESE MEAL POO

NICE AT THE TIME BUT ULTIMATELY UNSATISFYING. YOU'LL FEEL LIKE ANOTHER ONE IN HALF AN HOUR.

# POO No.23

# THE McBURGER POO

DRY, OVERCOOKED AND EACH POO IS IDENTICAL. WARNING: MAY CONTAIN TEENAGE STAFF'S BOGIES.

## POO No.24

# THE FISH + CHIPS POO

A SUCCULENT POO WITH A CRISP OUTER COATING. FOLLOWED BY A SIDE PORTION OF MUSHY PEE POO!

# POO No.25

# THE KEBAB POO

FOUL SMELLING, SLIMY, GROTESQUE APPEARANCE. JUST LIKE A KEBAB, REALLY!

JUDGING BY ALL THE 'CHOCOLATE KISSES' ON THE FLOOR, THE DOG'S BUM WAS IN NEED OF A WASH AGAIN.

JEFF COULDN'T
UNDERSTAND WHY
MAUDE REFUSED
TO SEE HIS
CHOCOLATE
STARFISH.

LILY FALLS INTO A HUGE CRACK IN THE PAVEMENT.

WHAT HAPPENS
WHEN YOU EAT
ONE TOO MANY
CURLY WURLIES.

BILLY CAME FIRST IN THE SWIMMING CONTEST THANKS TO THAT VINDALOO THE NIGHT BEFORE.

WHY IT'S
IMPORTANT NOT
TO BLOW OFF
IN THE DOGGY
POSITION.

ONCE AGAIN,
BILLY'S GOLDFISH
HAD DIARRHOEA.

HAVING FAILED TO FLUSH THE POO AWAY, MAUDE DECIDES TO SAVE EMBARRASSMENT AND HIDES IT IN HER HANDBAG.

NEVER CROSS
A PARK IN HIGH
HEELS.

APPARENTLY,
THE DOG HAD
SWALLOWED
AN ICING BAG
NOZZLE.

ONCE AGAIN,
BILLY'S PET
WORM WAS
CONSTIPATED.

ONE MORE CURRY
LIKE THAT ONE
LAST NIGHT AND
JEFF WOULD HAVE
TO FIT THE
TOILET WITH A
SEATBELT.

BILLY IMPRESSES
THE OTHER KIDS
WITH HIS VERY
OWN 'POO BEAR'.

THANKS TO JEFF,
NEVER AGAIN
WOULD POO
BECOME STUCK
TO THE DOG'S
BOTTY HAIR.

ONCE AGAIN,
MAUDE HAD V.P.L.
(VISIBLE
POO LINE).

# WHY IT'S IMPORTANT TO ALWAYS SIT AT THE FRONT ON ROLLER COASTERS.

MAUDE HAD
ACTUALLY SAID
SHE WANTED TO
DO SOMETHING
KINKY IN BED.

WELL, THAT WOULD BE THE LAST TIME BILLY WOULD ROLL DOWN A HILL WITH CAREFREE ABANDON.

JEFF ENTERS
ANOTHER
'WIPE IT OR
LEAVE IT'
DILEMMA.

JUST AS BILLY FINISHED HIS POO, THE TOILET PAPER RAN OUT.

AT THE DOCTOR'S, JEFF RECEIVES AN ANAL EXAMINATION.